EXPLORING THEATER

Hair and Makeup in Theater

Bethany Bryan

Cavendish Square
New York

Published in 2018 by Cavendish Square Publishing, LLC
243 5th Avenue, Suite 136, New York, NY 10016

First Edition

Website: cavendishsq.com

Library of Congress Cataloging-in-Publication Data

Names: Bryan, Bethany.
Title: Hair and makeup in theater / Bethany Bryan.
Description: New York : Cavendish Square, 2018. | Series: Exploring theater | Includes glossary and index. | Audience: Grades 7-12.
Identifiers: ISBN 9781502630032 (library bound) | ISBN 9781502634276 (pbk.) | ISBN 9781502630049 (ebook)
Subjects: LCSH: Theatrical makeup--Juvenile literature. | Hairdressing--Juvenile literature.
Classification: LCC PN2068.B78 2018 | DDC 792.02'7023--dc23

Editorial Director: David McNamara
Editor: Fletcher Doyle
Copy Editor: Nathan Heidelberger
Associate Art Director: Amy Greenan
Designer: Jessica Nevins
Production Coordinator: Karol Szymczuk
Photo Research: J8 Media

The photographs in this book are used by permission and through the courtesy of: Front cover, Frederick Florin/AFP/Getty Images; p. 4 Lev Radin/Shutterstock.com; p. 7 RyC - Behind The Lens (https://www.flickr.com/people/12665318@N07) from SanFrancisco, USA/File: Comikaze 2014 Anime cosplay (15546731037) .jpg/Wikimedia Commons; p. 9 Brenda Carson/Shutterstock.com; p. 13 GeorgeClerk/E+/Getty Images; pp. 17, 34, 65 Bruce Glikas/FilmMagic/Getty Images; p. 20 DEA Picture Library/De Agostini/Getty Images; p. 23 Lukovskii Andrei/Shutterstock.com; p. 26 Lane Turner/The Boston Globe/Getty Images; p. 28 Hill Street Studios/Blend Images/Getty Images; p. 31 Rawpixel.com/Shutterstock.com; pp. 37, 40, 57 Helene Pambrun/Paris Match/Getty Images; p. 44 Y Photo Studio/Shutterstock.com; p. 47 Mary Turner/Getty Images; p. 49 Don Arnold/WireImage/Getty Images; p. 52 Vladimir Gjorgiev/Shutterstock.com; p. 55 TomWargacki/WireImage/Getty Images; p. 58 Inmagineasia/Getty Images; p. 62 RichardCorkery/NY Daily News Archive/Getty Images; p. 67 Photofusion/UIG/Getty Images; p.70 Gary Friedman/Los Angeles Times/Getty Images; p. 72 JP Yim/Getty Images for Kenra Professional; p. 75 Bill Sykes/Cultura/Getty Images; p. 77 Shepel Nikolay/Wedding Photography/Shutterstock.com; p. 79 John Clutterbuck/DigitalVision/Getty Images; p. 84 Hero Images/Getty Images.

Printed in the United States of America

CONTENTS

Chapter 1:	Playing Dress-Up	5
Chapter 2:	Playing Your Role	16
Chapter 3:	The Steps of Staging a Production	28
Chapter 4:	When Things Go Wrong	58
Chapter 5:	Out in the World	73
Glossary		87
For More Information		90
Index		93
About the Author		96

Actor Billy Porter (*left*) underwent multiple wig and makeup changes every show.

CHAPTER ONE

Playing Dress-Up

The Broadway musical *Kinky Boots* debuted in 2013, starring actor Billy Porter as Lola, a drag queen who can't seem to find shoes that work well for her act, fit, or support her weight as she performs. Enter the local shoe factory owner, Charlie, whose business is failing. The two meet, and the shoe business undergoes a radical transformation as Charlie's factory starts making shoes fit for drag queens. The show went on to win six Tony Awards in 2013, including one for best lead actor, Billy Porter.

While Porter was clearly the star of the show, the wigs and makeup that helped complete his transformation into Lola were perfected down to a science. Onstage, under hot theater lights where the temperature can be well over 100 degrees Fahrenheit (38 degrees Celsius), Lola couldn't have her face melting away. Makeup artists had to find the right products and the right application to keep the makeup in place while not ruining Billy Porter's complexion. The makeup also had to be removed and reapplied several times over the course of the show, with Lola changing in and out of her stage persona. There were also around eighty wigs worn by Lola and the show's other drag queens. The wigs required so much special care that they had their own staff. The wigs had to be styled before every performance, whether this involved pinning a curl to keep it in place or diving into the fray with a hot curling iron. Because of the crew's planning and coordination, the longest transformation from Billy to Lola only took eleven minutes.

The hair and makeup that brings a character to life onstage is an essential part of an actor's costume. Makeup not only transforms a man into Rum Tum Tugger for a performance of *Cats*, it also accentuates the actors' faces so that the audience can read their expressions more clearly, even from the seat farthest from the stage. A simple victory roll can take an actress's modern hairstyle and turn her into a 1940s pinup, and a good wig can transform an actor into almost anything or anyone. All it takes is skill, time, and a lot of dedication.

Hair and Makeup and You

As a high school student, you've likely taken part in a theater performance, either onstage or behind the scenes. And if you haven't been onstage, you've definitely put on a costume at Halloween or cosplayed as your favorite character at a comics convention.

Getting into a costume, donning a wig, and putting on a swipe of black-as-night lipstick might feel totally natural to you. If so, you might enjoy working with hair and makeup as part of a theater production. You might even consider it to be a good career option for the future. If you know you love the

Cosplayers often use wigs and makeup to transform themselves into their favorite characters from TV, comics, video games, anime, and more.

theater, but you haven't quite found your niche, that's OK, too. There are a lot of ways to be involved with the theater. Hair and makeup is just one of them!

The good news is that the skills required for working with hair and makeup are simply an interest in hair and makeup, and some chutzpah to make your dreams come true. Anyone with the willingness and patience to learn can train to be a stylist for the stage.

When it comes to makeup, there is a lot to know beyond just application. You have to know a little bit about general skin care. If an actor has a naturally oily complexion, you might want to find a particular brand of **foundation** that won't exacerbate the problem and cause breakouts. An actor who suffers from **rosacea**, a natural redness of the skin, needs his or her makeup applied in a manner that helps cover the redness. Every actor's skin is different, and each one will have different needs. A good makeup artist will come prepared for that. Luckily, there are classes that you can take online to help get the training you need, but many makeup artists are self-taught. All of the different makeup trends and products are changing daily, so you'll want to follow popular beauty blogs and YouTube channels dedicated to all things makeup. You may even want to start a channel or blog of your own to get your name out there before you even leave high school.

As a makeup artist for the stage, you'll also need to know a little something about makeup styles throughout history and ways to imitate them using modern makeup products. You'll want to understand how makeup has changed, even over the past decade,

Makeup, hair, and costumes might be elaborate or simple.

and know how to recreate a look. Luckily, the internet is full of classic makeup looks to use as an inspiration. There are also theater history courses available at the college level that might provide some extra insight.

Creativity is an important part of being a makeup artist. A **director** for a theater production might have a particular look for the performance in mind,

MAKEUP ... ON ME?

If you're a guy, you might be thinking, "Makeup? On me? No way." Perhaps it's because makeup seems like something that's exclusively for girls. (Even if you are a girl or gender nonconforming, you might feel some trepidation about putting on makeup because it doesn't feel quite "you.") Historically, makeup has been worn by males and females. King Tutankhamun wore black kohl liner around his eyes. Englishmen of the eighteenth century were frequently found wearing makeup to whiten their skin and rouge their cheeks. Today, celebrities like Johnny Depp, Jared Leto, and Russell Brand have made wearing makeup part of their daily routine. David Bowie built his career around his makeup-wearing alter ego Ziggy Stardust. Makeup is cool, it's transformative, and it opens up the wearer for a lot of possibilities on the stage.

Thespis, an actor in ancient Greece, was one of the first men to wear makeup onstage. He wanted to

and it is your role to find ways to make that look a reality, using only makeup. The look might be subtle, or it might be dramatic. It might be your job to age a character thirty years or make her look sick. Within the budget you are given, how can you find ways to achieve that particular look? Sometimes all it takes is a creative approach.

stand out from the Greek chorus. The Peking Opera has been around since the 1600s, with actors using heavy swirls of black, red, blue, and white makeup to help convey to the audience what motivates their character. Since men played all of the parts in Shakespeare's England, to prepare for female roles, the actors painted their faces pale with makeup made from powdered hogs' bones mixed with poppy oil.

If you're headed to the stage for the first time and you're nervous about wearing makeup, it's OK. There are a lot of online tutorials about how to apply stage makeup to all different types of faces. Get a friend who is a makeup expert and have him or her help you with the application. After a while, putting on makeup to prepare for a show will feel totally normal. Just be sure to wash your face well after the performance and apply some moisturizer. Heavy stage makeup has been known to cause breakouts!

You will also need to know how to work as part of a team. You will be working alongside the director, actors, **costume designer**, set designer, and more. And you'll all be working within a limited timeline. It's important to know when to share your ideas and when to listen to other people's ideas. You may find yourself working alongside people who don't deliver criticism constructively or who seem to change their minds daily. Learning how to deal with any number of unforeseen situations is an important skill.

Hair Know-How

When it comes to styling hair for the stage, there is a lot to know and a lot to learn for an aspiring stylist. Sometimes stylists will have the ability to work with an actor's real hair, if it can be styled appropriately or doesn't require a specific look. Sometimes a quick and simple change to an existing hairstyle can be made between acts. Other times, to achieve a specific look, a stylist might require the use of a wig or a variety of wigs. Therefore, the most important skill that an aspiring stylist can acquire is some "hair know-how."

Different types and textures of hair require different techniques. Is it easier to achieve a certain look when the hair is wet or dry, dirty or clean? Which products are best to use to keep every hair in place from the moment the actors take the stage to their final bow? Do you know your victory rolls from your French twists? These are things you learn through time, research, and practice. You can experiment with different hairstyles on your friends and family members, even on yourself. Styling a wig can be a very similar experience, without the body accompanying the hairstyle. The type of fibers used to make the wig will determine how you style, clean, and maintain a wig, so a firm knowledge of wigs is important as well.

An aspiring hair stylist will also need to be extremely organized. Most theaters will have a

The stylist knows the right technique to use to get the hair of this young actor ready for the performance.

collection of wigs that have been used in previous productions. Keeping the wigs organized so that they can be easily located and assigned to each actor is important. So is knowing when a hairstyle or wig needs to change mid-performance and finding the best way to get the job done seamlessly.

As with the skills required for an aspiring makeup artist, a hair stylist will need to be able to work well with others and be prepared to work within a specific deadline and budget.

Getting Involved

One of the best ways to gain some experience and extra skill, whether you are interested in hair, makeup, or both, is to jump right in and volunteer to work on a theater production. Your school might have a **drama club**, so get involved with that if you can. If there isn't a drama club, check into starting one. Pass around a sign-up sheet to gauge the interest of other students, post flyers, talk to your English or music teacher to see if they would be willing to be your faculty sponsor, or start a group on **social media** to talk about your plan with your fellow students. You'll be surprised how many other students will want to join.

There might also be a local community theater near you in need of volunteers. Some community theaters will even let volunteers sign up online. Don't lose heart if they don't specifically need volunteers to help with hair and makeup. Building sets, making costumes, or even passing out **playbills** is a great way to just get backstage and learn the process of staging a performance. You never know what you might learn. And if you can show yourself to be a capable volunteer for one production, you'll definitely be invited back for the next production.

If a theater doesn't exist in your area, then it might be up to you to find a way to showcase your talents. Make a movie or web series with a group of friends and a video camera. Check with your local department of parks and recreation to find out about potential venues that might be available for free or for a small fee and might be open to a group of young performers to stage a production. (They might require that you apply for a permit, so keep that in mind.)

There are other ways to gain experience with makeup. Department stores need people who understand makeup and can apply it to customers to sell products. Fashion shows also need people skilled with makeup. Hair salons can provide training in styling and dealing with different types of hair. You might have to get a little bit creative to make your theater dreams a reality, but it will be worth it.

CHAPTER TWO

Playing Your Role

Teamwork is possibly the most important aspect of staging a theater production. Everyone onstage and behind the scenes plays an important role. To keep the performance running smoothly, everyone must do his or her part, both individually and as part of the team. For this to work, you will want to not only know how to do your job well, but the jobs of everyone around you. If you're in charge of Elphaba's makeup in *Wicked*, who in lighting is in charge of making sure that makeup really "pops" onstage? Who can you talk to about an important costume change and how it will affect how you style a character's wig for the second act? Teamwork brings all of these elements together and helps your vision come to life.

Team Goals

As a stage production begins to take shape, you'll find yourself working alongside people who will be a big part of your life for the next several weeks or months. This is your team, and it is helpful to start thinking

Jimmy Cortes (makeup), Kathe Mull (dresser), and Chris Clark (hair) helped actress Kerry Ellis bring Elphaba to life.

of them that way. You will have to learn to rely on each other to get stuff done and solve problems, both large and small. If the production is a large one, hair and makeup might be handled by separate teams. If the production is small, hair and makeup might be one group, which may even be part of the costume department.

The first thing a team must figure out is who is in charge. Is it an older student, parent volunteer, or member of your school's faculty? This is an important person to know. A good leader will keep things running smoothly and delegate tasks to everyone within your team.

If you're the one in charge, make sure you get to know everyone on your team. Introduce yourself to anyone you don't already know, and remember that if everyone on your team is happy, they will do a better job. Make sure that everyone feels valued and appreciated, and you'll be off to a great start. One of the first things you might want to do is talk to the individual members of your team about their particular interests or talents. A longtime cosplayer who has dabbled in special effects makeup might be well suited for a complicated makeup design that requires more skill. An amateur hair stylist who can work quickly and efficiently and seems to handle stress well may be your go-to stylist for a fast hairstyle change. Team members who are less sure of their skills and need a little more guidance can be delegated to roles that will allow them to shadow a more experienced member of the team.

Costumes, Hair, and Makeup

Costumes, hair, and makeup go together like peanut butter, jelly, and bread. These three groups (or departments, in the case of a larger or professional production) work together to help create a specific "look" for each character in a production. Early in the process, team leaders will sit down to discuss their vision for the production. This vision will need to coincide with the director's vision. Meetings are a big part of teamwork early in a theater production, so no matter your role in the production, be ready to be on time, and write your ideas out in advance so you don't forget anything.

The head of a costume department is usually referred to as the costume designer or head of wardrobe. This individual will design a look for each

This is one of Marcel Multzer's sketches for the first production of the opera *Carmen* in 1875.

of the main characters in the show after discussing the overall look of the production with the director and set designer. Then the costume designer will meet with the hair and makeup departments to go over the designs and find ways to enhance the look with hair and makeup. If you are working on hair and makeup for a theater production, your work will be closely linked to the costume department from the show's inception to its close. While the costume department is hard at work finding just the right hat for Dolly Levi—the title character of the musical *Hello, Dolly!*—you can be sure that they're being mindful of the wig or hairstyle Dolly will be wearing under that hat. Communication between departments is key. Let's take a look at everyone else you might encounter as part of the hair and makeup team for a theater production.

Hair and Makeup Designer

In a college-level or professional production, the theater may employ a hair and makeup designer. It is that person's job to work with the costume department to design a look for all of the lead actors and key members of the **chorus** (or background players). This individual will study the script carefully and commit some hairstyle and makeup designs to paper (or computer), being mindful of the play's time period and the vision of the director. The designer's vision needs to be both creative and practical, as a look must be functional. As tempting as it might be to use extra-gruesome **prostheses** to make the

Phantom of the Opera as hideous as possible under his mask, the actor has to be able to sing for the length of the performance with that makeup. A hair and makeup designer must take every possibility into consideration and plan accordingly.

Makeup Artist

Once a makeup design is approved, it is the job of a theatrical makeup artist to bring the look to life—and to do so for every performance. Large, well-funded theaters will hire professional makeup artists—either full-time or on a freelance basis—while smaller or community-run theaters might rely on volunteer makeup artists. Volunteers might work for free in order to build a professional makeup **portfolio**. (It is important to note that, in many states, you must be a licensed cosmetologist to apply makeup professionally, but many makeup artists are self-taught.) Makeup artists often gain experience by practicing on friends or relatives or doing makeup for weddings or other special occasions. In addition to applying makeup before every performance, a makeup artist must be knowledgeable about skin care in order to prevent reactions to certain chemicals in makeup. Makeup artists usually bring their own **makeup kit**, which is a large investment that can be added to over time.

Professional makeup artists must keep brushes clean and replace expired makeup in their kits in order to keep actors safe from infection. Not only does the makeup artist have to be mindful of finding the right shade of foundation for an actor's skin or a good eye pencil for just the right cat's eye, he or she must plan the application of the makeup. Does the makeup need to last for the entire performance, or will it need to be removed within an hour? Which products will best accommodate a fast makeup change or stay on for all three hours of the performance? These are things a makeup artist must consider. After a performance has ended, it is also often the job of a makeup artist to remove the makeup or instruct an actor on removing makeup in a way that doesn't lead to a skin breakout or inflammation in the future.

Hair and/or Wig Stylist

A production that requires the use of several wigs will often employ wig stylists whose job is to maintain and style the wigs, and help with wig changes during a performance. Wig stylists show up several hours before a performance and begin to prepare the wigs for the show, adding fresh curls, pinning a lock of hair so that it stays out of an actor's face, and checking the wig for any damage. (Luckily for the actors, wigs can be styled on wig stands, which are made to hold a wig upright when it is not being worn.) When it's time for an actor to put on a wig, a hair or wig stylist will help secure a **wig cap** to the actor's head. A wig cap is made from nylon (often old nylon hose), which helps protect both the natural hair underneath and the wig itself, as well as the actor's scalp. (Wigs can be itchy!) It also helps to keep a wig on the head once it's pinned in place. In some musicals, wigs must also accommodate carefully hidden microphones and

Wigs can provide historical context to a stage production.

THE FUNCTION OF A COSTUME DESIGN

To the untrained eye, a character's costume might just seem like an appropriate choice of outfit. But a costume does a lot more than simply give an actor something to wear. A costume also helps to:

- Convey the mood of a production. A dark, somber costume in a play by Henrik Ibsen will give people in the audience the sense that the play will be dark and somber, even if they are not familiar with the themes of Ibsen's work.
- Help a character stand out among the others. If there are five actors onstage, and four of them are wearing dark colors and one is wearing red, the one wearing red will seem the most significant, as in a production of *Annie.*
- Change an actor's appearance. In a production of *The Magic Flute,* an opera composed by Mozart, costume designers often want the

wires. As an actor finishes with a wig, it's the job of the stylist to clean and prepare the wig for the next performance. Some wigs, particularly ones made out of real human hair, can cost thousands of dollars, so keeping them clean and undamaged is important.

A hair stylist's job often includes styling wigs and/or an actor's actual hair before a performance.

Queen of the Night character to transcend humanness so that her every appearance onstage is intense, memorable, and dramatic.

- Indicate character development and the passage of time. In 2013, as the TV show *Breaking Bad* drew to the end of its final season, the website TDYLF shared an infographic it had made, revealing how the show's producers had used the color of the characters' costumes to reflect how each of them had changed throughout the show's progression. A character who had become more evil lost his color, moving slowly to a more neutral color scheme, while a character who had become stronger and more independent over the seasons is dressed more colorfully in each episode. The changes were so subtle viewers would not notice a difference right away.

Hair stylists often practice a particular hairstyle on an actor in advance so that the styling process can be streamlined for speed and efficiency. In a large professional performance, an actor might have a hair stylist whose job is to style only him or her. In a small theater, one person may style everyone or teach actors how to recreate a look on their own.

Students must balance homework with rehearsals and other activities.

Being a Good Team Member

Before you've joined the hair and makeup team for a theater production, you must ensure you can be a good, responsible member of the team. As a high school student, you'll often find you will have to

juggle schoolwork, family obligations, and your job with rehearsals or planning meetings. So sit down and plan out a strategy for handling the workload. One Friday night, you might have to meet with the costume designer when your mind is on that big English paper that's due Monday, so sometimes you can start to feel overwhelmed. Don't waste any spare time. You might be able to do homework during rehearsal downtime or take some time during homeroom to draw up some makeup designs. If you're determined to make it as a theatrical makeup artist, makeup designer, hair stylist, or whatever your theater dream might be, you'll find opportunities to take care of your responsibilities so you can showcase your talents in the theater.

CHAPTER THREE

The Steps of Staging a Production

There are three steps involved with staging a production: preproduction, rehearsal, and show time. Preproduction allows the theater company or group staging the production time to plan a budget, acquire any licenses required to stage a particular play or musical (or other type of performance), hire a director and members of the stage crew, plan for and conduct auditions, and select the cast, in addition to a multitude of other tasks. During rehearsals, the stage crew designs and builds the sets; costumes are designed, sourced, and made; and actors learn and memorize their lines, in addition to any music, lyrics, or dance steps. In short, cast and crew prepare everything to put on a show. At show time, audience members at last get to see the final product! As they enjoy the show, the crew is backstage making sure that everything goes off without a hitch. Even with a great deal of work behind them, cast and stage crew continue working hard, even after the last curtain falls on the final performance.

While it might seem like the hair and makeup crews involved in a theater production have a pretty simple job—applying an actor's lipstick or pinning

The time onstage comprises just a small portion of the work involved in putting on a production.

a wig in place before a performance—there is a lot more to it than that. Everything must go off without a hitch, and that requires planning and foresight. Let's take a look at what the hair and makeup crews are up to during each step of a stage production.

Hair and Makeup Preproduction

A theater company decides to stage a production. The project has a producer or producers, and the project has a set budget. The theater's artistic director has a vision for a dark, gritty interpretation of one of Shakespeare's tragedies. Or she envisions a bright, flashy production of a musical that was formerly a big hit on Broadway and will likely bring in a large audience and sell out all performances. The show officially enters the preproduction stage. A costume designer is hired. He or she has a vision of color and simplicity. Now it's time for a hair and makeup designer to come on board and take on the important role of planning a "look" for the characters.

A theater's budget for hair and makeup may be as little as a few hundred dollars to as much as a few million dollars. If you've worked in hair and makeup on a high school or local theater production, you might know that sometimes there's no budget for it at all. How a show is budgeted, who is hired to do what, and how many people can be brought in varies from show to show and theater to theater. If the budget is high and if costumes are elaborate, requiring hair and makeup design to help bring the whole thing together, often an individual hair designer and makeup designer will be brought on board. Sometimes those designers will be one and the same. (We'll discuss the role here as if one person is performing both jobs.)

Once a hair and makeup designer is brought on, he or she will meet with other members of the crew to begin to formulate a plan. According to the Simpson College theater department website, a hair and makeup designer will first read over the script and work with the costume designer to begin to create a costume breakdown for the entire performance. The designer will draw up some sketches to share, collaborating with stage management in order to ensure ease of transition between costumes and to make sure that the production's vision is maintained. If a play has a specific historical setting, a hair and makeup designer will need to be mindful of historical

During preproduction, the costumes, hair, and makeup crews will create designs for every character.

and cultural accuracy. Research is a big part of being a hair and makeup designer. Many designers have a library of go-to resources, often kept in the theater so they can be accessed as needed.

A hair and makeup designer will also work with costumes and other departments in order to figure out a hair and makeup budget. Does the theater have wigs, makeup, and other supplies at the ready, or will other items need to be purchased? Who will be in charge of purchasing those items?

Meetings are a very important part of any stage production. **Budget meetings** help crewmembers and department heads come up with individual department budgets, allotting available funds where they are needed most. Creative (or design) meetings allow members of different departments to share and collaborate on creative ideas. And meetings take place as frequently as time will allow in order to get every little element squared away. Several meetings a week are common. A hair and makeup designer might also attend actor auditions or callbacks in some cases.

Once a design is completed, the hair and makeup designer will share color copies of the final design with the director, stage manager, **costume shop** manager or costume designer, and lighting designer. A designer might also be expected to formally present the design to the cast and other members of the crew. A hair and makeup designer may also be in charge of hiring his or her own team of wig/hair stylists and makeup artists as part of his or her preproduction tasks. Stylists and makeup artists will usually come on board around the same time that acting parts are cast.

If wig stylists or makeup artists are around during preproduction, they might be found in the costume shop—where all costume materials, including clothing, jewelry, hats, costume props, wigs, and other costume accessories, are kept—checking out what's available, putting together a list of things they will need, or meeting with the hair and makeup designer to collaborate on some design ideas. Most stylists and makeup artists, however, aren't really needed until the show is cast. That's when their work begins, for the most part.

Rehearsal for Everyone

As rehearsals begin, a hair and makeup designer's workload might change a little. With an approved design in the bag, the hair and makeup designer—often coordinating with the costume department—will begin to assign specific tasks to the members of the crew. All departments, including hair and makeup, will come together for frequent production meetings. These meetings are just a way of sharing information among different departments. If you spend all of your time in the costume shop, you won't have much time to have a chat with lighting on a daily basis. Production meetings bring all departments together to help keep things running smoothly.

Rehearsals aren't just a chance for actors to run their lines. They're for everyone involved in a production. A hair and makeup designer might take this time to watch the actors onstage to see what's working and what isn't, and how this will affect the hair and makeup design. It also provides an opportunity for a designer to read along in the script, take notes, and get familiar with the cues.

Rehearsals for Hair

During the rehearsal stage, a wig stylist, often working alongside a member of the costume crew, will head into the costume shop and begin to pull wigs from the available stock. Most items in the costume shop were used in previous productions. Since theaters have limited budgets, the costume shop

ANGELINA AVALLONE, MAKEUP DESIGNER

Angelina Avallone was once a model and fashion student living in Florence, Italy. However, she always loved the process of creating. She studied costume design at Yale and, afterwards, dedicated her life to

Angelina Avallone (*right*, with wig designer Paul Huntley) pulls inspiration from a variety of places.

working in the theater. Becoming a makeup stylist, Avallone was responsible for designing the monster in the Broadway production of *Young Frankenstein* and Ursula in *The Little Mermaid.*

When coming up with a makeup design for the Grinch in *Dr. Seuss's How the Grinch Stole Christmas,* Avallone wanted to do something a little different. In an article she wrote for Broadway.com, she said, "Jim Carrey played the Grinch on film in full prosthetics, but we wanted to avoid that because it would limit Patrick Page's facial expressions. Robert Morgan designed a wonderful fur costume with knobby knees, a belly, Grinch-like elbows and gloves with long fingers, so we thought, okay, let's not completely cover up this actor. Let's see if we can do this so he can use every muscle on his face."

She said to the website Into the Gloss of her experience of working on the Broadway revival of *Cabaret,* "Makeup design starts with research. For this production of *Cabaret* I wanted to go back to source material rather than reference what somebody did twenty years ago. We looked at books, photos of real people, photos of movie stars—Spring 1930, what were the German fashion magazines? It's about going back and looking at *Vogue* ads or cabaret posters from that time, painters of that period, photographers, trying to find actual *makeup* from that period."

manager will very often salvage and reuse anything and everything. This includes wigs. The stylist will then assess what can be done to make a wig "work" for a particular character and actor. A quality wig can be styled a variety of ways, even trimmed and repurposed (by an experienced hair or wig stylist) to fit a production's specific needs. If the costume shop doesn't have the necessary wig or something that can be made to work, a wig stylist will have to purchase, borrow, beg, or rent one, being mindful of the budget, which is almost always a part of the costumes budget. (A purchased wig will go into the costume shop stock to be used for future performances once the production ends. Every purchase is an investment in future productions.)

Wig stylists will often schedule a moment with an actor to have him or her try on a wig. It's not uncommon to see members of the hair and makeup department waiting with a wig in the wings during a rehearsal for a moment of an actor's time. Once a wig has been selected, fitted, and approved by the costume designer/hair and makeup designer, it will be stored among the other materials assigned to a specific actor and tagged accordingly. If the costume shop keeps a log of costume pieces, someone in the department might update the database to assign a specific piece to a specific actor. Every costume shop is different in terms of organization. It's a good idea to familiarize yourself with the system of organization at every theater at which you work.

A hair stylist can also double as a wig stylist. They can be one and the same or different people with vastly different roles, depending on the production,

Wig stylists often show up hours before a performance starts to curl, comb, clean, and repair wigs.

the theater, the budget, and any other number of factors. If an actor will go onstage with his or her own hair, a hair stylist will often schedule time to meet with him or her and try out some styles to see what will work. This is also a great time for a quick skin test to make sure that the actor will not have a reaction to any chemicals in the wig adhesives or the wig itself. Test adhesives behind the ear, using a Q-tip. If that skin or the skin under the wig becomes red and irritated, the actor is having a reaction. Switch to a hypoallergenic wig tape or swap out the wig. The rehearsal period is actually a perfect time for hair and wig stylists to "rehearse" a style, see how quickly it can be done, and do some style-change test runs to see how much time it will take. Hairstyles for the stage must work well with every element of an actor's costume, including hats or headpieces.

Hair 101

Most professional theater productions will hire a licensed hair or wig stylist. A community theater might not be able to afford one, in which case they might rely on volunteer hair stylists. A hair stylist new to working on stage hair will want to learn the basics before going into the rehearsal stage and beginning to interact with the actors and formulating a hairstyle plan.

First to consider is whether the actor will require a wig or if his or her hair can be styled appropriately. If the show requires hairstyle changes, you might want to opt for using a few wigs that can be styled in advance. If one hairstyle will do and the actor's hair can be styled in a manner that is functional and appropriate, you may choose to go in that direction.

Simplicity, unless the script calls for something extraordinary—*Hedwig and the Angry Inch*, for example, requires several elaborate hairstyles—is usually the best rule of thumb when styling hair for a stage production. You don't want an actor's hairstyle to distract from his or her acting. It's also important to ask an actor what he or she wants and what he or she is comfortable with in terms of hairstyles. Most actors like to have some say in how their character will look onstage since they are the ones presenting the character to the audience. It's a great idea to walk into a first meeting with an actor with a design in hand and a solid plan for how the design will be carried out. Then listen to any suggestions or preferences. It's important to let an actor know how much time he or she will spend having his or her hair styled before each performance—and how much time it will take, later on, to remove the costume.

Styling hair for the theater requires a lot of research at times. If you are looking for something really unique and bold or a look that is relevant to a certain time period, the internet is a great resource. Hair stylists post step-by-step style tutorials on YouTube.

You'll also want to familiarize yourself with different lengths and textures of hair. Styling coarse, curly hair is very different from styling thin, straight hair. Each type of hair requires different tools. Be sure to keep a variety of combs on hand, and familiarize yourself with each type. A tail comb is best for parting and sectioning hair because it does precise work. Wide-tooth combs are best for thick, curly hair as they won't tangle in the hair as easily. An afro hair comb or pick is best for African American hair.

You will also want a firm understanding of the different sizes and styles of bobby pins, hairpins, rollers, and styling tools such as curling and straightening irons and blow dryers. Investing in a curling or straightening iron that has an auto-shutoff function is a great idea because you never know how quickly you will be distracted, jumping from one hairstyle to the next before a performance. A blow dryer with a diffuser attachment and a concentrator attachment that can be swapped out as necessary is

These stylists work hard to prepare the actors for their performance of *The Legend of King Arthur* in 2016.

also a great investment. This allows you to use one tool for many tasks.

Remember that the decisions that you make as a hair stylist will speak volumes about a character before he or she even opens his or her mouth. Messy, unkempt hair reflects a chaotic life and lifestyle. Neat, tidy hairstyles might make the audience feel like a character is very organized, perhaps even to a fault. Curly hair might convey a sense of wildness and fun, while straight hair might make a character seem more prim and proper. The same goes for accessories. A neatly tied hair bow says one thing about a character, while one that has come untied and trails down the back says another. So it's very important to step back and ask yourself, "What does this hairstyle say?" Once you've completed a look for a character, be sure to take a quality picture so that you will be able to add it to your portfolio.

Facial Hair Styling

Hair styling also includes any facial hair—beards, mustaches, eyebrows, sideburns, etc. Facial hair might be fake and applied using **spirit gum**, a special adhesive that is safe for skin application.

There are a few types of fake facial hair. The first is a ready-made mustache, beard, or other type of facial hair that has been styled and simply has to be glued on the face or attached using adhesive tape. (There are fake beards that attach to the ears using elastic or hooks, but you want a more foolproof method of attaching the beard for a theater production.) More realistic beards are woven using a special type of lace. These are attached using spirit gum and can be trimmed, if necessary, to adjust the style. (These can be expensive, so leave any trimming to an experienced stylist.) You can also simply apply loose strands of fake hair to the face using spirit gum. This is a good application technique if the actor simply needs the appearance of stubble or a light beard.

Facial hair color should match wig hair or natural hair as closely as possible. If a wig is being repurposed or trimmed anyway, you might want to hang on to any trimmings and repurpose those for facial hair. This is a great way to make sure that the hair colors will match. Additionally, wigs or false facial hair can often be dyed to match another shade. Just be sure that the product is safe to use with dye. Plastic-based fake hair will not take color as well as real hair or hair made from organic materials.

Facial hair worn on the stage might also be real, on some occasions. When *Fiddler on the Roof* was revived on Broadway in 2015–2016, many of the actors grew and maintained their own beards rather than opting to wear fake facial hair, according to an article on the TheaterMania website. The downside of this is that an actor must keep the beard even when it starts getting hot outside. If a cast member decides to grow and maintain his own beard, you might consider adding a beard trimmer to your styling kit, as well as an appropriate balm or wax.

Facial hair is part of a costume and sometimes requires just as much forethought as a wig. Again, the internet is a great resource for checking out beard, mustache, and sideburn styles throughout history.

Rehearsals for Makeup

As with hair and wigs, makeup artists also need a moment to "rehearse" a look. Makeup artists often practice elaborate or complicated makeup designs on themselves, volunteers, or friends before trying them out on the actors. If an actor has sensitive skin or skin prone to breakouts, a makeup artist will often experiment with a variety of products to get just the right blend. If a show requires a makeup special effect, a makeup artist will begin to find or create any necessary prostheses—noses, whiskers, scars, etc.

Many of these items are crafted for a specific actor using latex. If you're new to making prostheses, there are resources online and in books to help you learn the process, but only practice, and a few failures, will truly teach you the art.

Once a makeup artist feels confident about a design, he or she will schedule time to "rehearse it" with the actor. This is especially necessary if the look is complicated, elaborate, or requires a lot of time to apply. The actor should feel comfortable speaking lines, singing, dancing—whatever is necessary—while wearing his character's makeup. If something isn't working, a makeup artist will go back and make any necessary changes to the plan.

Says makeup artist Lindsey Bacon, "The great thing about makeup for theater is that you get a few **dress rehearsals** to test out how your looks will fare under the lighting before the audience will see your work. You also have the whole run of the show to tweak the looks you've designed until they're perfect." An artist's work is never done.

Makeup Know-How

Theater makeup is very different from the type of makeup people use every day. "Makeup for theater is much more like painting," says Bacon, "and your imagination is the limit."

Makeup for the theater is not an exact science. Nor can it be bound by any limits to creativity. If you think you can do it, you can do it.

If you wear makeup yourself, chances are you know every little thing about your face—how to

Makeup application for the stage can be as elaborate as it needs to be to bring a character to life.

contour your nose just the right way, which cheek stain to use with your skin tone, the right lip color for everything you do with your eyes. But, as a makeup artist, it's important to understand every type of face and every skin tone. You should familiarize yourself with applying makeup to different eye shapes. Deep-set, monolid, hooded, and protruding eye shapes (among others) all require very specific makeup application styles. Read up on each, and practice applying makeup on different eye shapes until you feel comfortable with the skill.

Theater makeup is not meant to make an actor look dreamy up close. It's meant to help an actor be seen from the audience and not look washed-out under the stage lights. If you are applying makeup for a stage performance for the first time, that's an important rule to follow. Application is simple if you keep that in mind.

Remember that, in most cases, theater makeup is meant to say something about a character, so it's important to keep that in mind as you begin. Pink or coral shades and a touch of highlight on the cheeks are going to convey youthfulness, while dark colors and rouge tend to come off as more mature.

First, start by having the actor wash his or her face. Then use a toner and moisturizer. Then you'll want to pick the right foundation to go with the actor's skin tone. It's a great idea to go "warm" with the tone and not too cool, unless the character is sick or a ghost. Blend the foundation in well, making sure to blend at the hairline and jawline. There should not be a stark contrast at these places between the makeup and natural skin tone. You'll also want to familiarize yourself with contouring. Most beauty stores sell contour palettes, which give you a selection of skin tone colors. Highlight the nose and cheeks with a lighter color and use a darker color around the nose and under the cheekbones to give the face more definition from a distance. Line the eyes with a dark color, black for a more dramatic look and brown for a more natural look. Draw in eyebrows using a pencil in a dark shade of black or brown. When you have created the desired effect, be sure to apply powder liberally (and use a setting spray, if you have one).

After each performance, remind actors to remove all makeup using a gentle cleanser and follow up with a moisturizer. Skin can be very sensitive after application and removal of heavy makeup.

Safety is extremely important when it comes to makeup application. Always wash brushes and other makeup applicators between uses on different actors. (Having several spares helps if you don't have time to wash your brushes and let them dry.) At least once a month, be sure to go through your supplies and discard and replace any makeup that is expired. Keeping your supplies clean and up to date helps reduce the spread of infection.

After each performance, your makeup kit will likely be in chaos. Always take the time to put everything back where it belongs and clean all of your makeup brushes thoroughly and set them out to dry in a clean, dry location.

Fake Eyelashes 101

Fake eyelashes fall into the responsibility of the makeup artist, unlike other types of fake facial hair. This is for a few reasons. First, fake eyelashes are usually part of a makeup design. Second, they require a gentler type of application and adhesive.

Different styles of fake eyelashes have been relevant at different times throughout history, so be sure to do your research before picking out a pair. The doe-eyed look of the 1950s was often created by using a half lash glued from the center of the lashes to the outer edge of the eye. In the 1960s, women

Fake eyelashes can be tricky to apply before you feel completely comfortable doing it yourself.

often wore more than one pair to capture the look of a thick, extravagant lash line.

Before applying a set of fake eyelashes, you might want to give them a quick trim. Natural eyelashes are shorter at the inner corner of the eye. You can also cut the lash into individual sections if you find that this makes them easier to apply. Mascara should be applied before lashes are glued to the lid, although you can make **touch-ups** afterward. Otherwise you run the risk of pulling the lash loose or irritating the eye. Other eye makeup should be applied first as well. Use only eyelash glue, never any other kind of adhesive. Apply a thin, even coat of glue to the base of the fake eyelashes and place them as close behind the natural lash line as you can. Secure the center first, followed by the inner corner, and finally—very gently—press down the outermost corner of the lash.

Fake eyelashes should be worn exclusively by one person, and they should be cleaned and dried after every use. Infections like conjunctivitis (pinkeye) can spread from one eye to another on fake eyelashes or on an unwashed hand.

Special Effects Makeup 101

Many of the same early steps of makeup application go for special effects makeup as well. Have the actor wash his or her face thoroughly. Apply any prostheses first. If you apply makeup before attaching a prosthetic nose, scar, or other facial enhancement, the adhesive won't work as well. Makeup is applied after that. As with a simpler makeup job, use powder or a setting spray to keep the final product from running or smearing.

Dress and Technical Rehearsals

In preparation for a show opening, there are rehearsals both with and without costumes. They all help wrap up any last issues before opening night.

At a **dress parade,** actors put on their costumes and stand before the costume designer and artistic director so that they'll have the chance to see everyone together. If, for instance, a specific color

Dress rehearsal allows actors to perform in makeup and costume before the first performance.

scheme has been chosen for the lead actor, and another actor is wearing that color during dress parade, the costume department will have the opportunity to make a change. As a member of the hair and makeup crew, you will almost definitely be required to attend the dress parade. Be prepared to take notes and write down any issues you'll need to address in the following days. Dress parade is also a great time to take pictures of styles for which you were responsible so that you can add them to your portfolio.

The dress rehearsal allows the actors to run through an entire performance in costume. Costume and hair and makeup crewmembers are on hand for dress rehearsal to help with costume changes, style changes, or quick fixes. The dress rehearsal is usually followed by a quick meeting that gives everyone involved in the production the chance to discuss and address any issues.

The **technical rehearsal** is a rehearsal during which the performers run through an entire performance, but the focus is on getting lighting and sound cues right. A dry tech rehearsal will include only crew and designers, no actors. Wet tech will include actors, but often they won't be required to be in costume. The hair and makeup department might still need to be on hand for the tech rehearsal, so be sure to check in with your head of department before taking that night off.

After each of these rehearsals, the hair and makeup and costume departments as a whole might sit down to discuss any last issues. Be sure to take notes during these rehearsals so that you don't forget any important information you might like to bring up during the meeting. Opening night is now just around the corner.

It's Show Time!

Several weeks of hard work have passed, and it's finally opening night. By this point, everyone—cast and crew—knows the parts that they will play, both onstage and off. First of all, congratulations! You made it to opening night—arguably the most important night of an entire theater production. Secondly, don't get comfortable just yet. There is still a lot to do.

Opening Night Hair and Wig Prep

If you arrive early for any performance night, let it be opening night. This is your chance to not only get a step ahead on your preshow prep, it also gives you a little extra time just in case anything goes wrong. On opening night, many members of the cast and crew are going to have the jitters. Actors are going to be hiding in the corner running lines one last time. They're going to be distracted and nervous. Giving yourself a little extra time will take some of the stress off of you as you try to do your job.

By opening night, you should have a system in place for how and in which order actors need to be styled. But it can't hurt to go over your to-do list one last time before you jump in to your preparation. Wigs can be styled before actors arrive, so focus on that first. Make sure that every wig is accompanied by a wig cap. Count wig caps twice to make sure you have enough of them, and then put two extras in your pocket, just in case.

As actors begin to arrive, focus on the most complicated hairstyles (usually those worn by women) first. You will need to coordinate the schedule with the costume and makeup departments. (Large, professional productions might also require that an actor wear a mic pack and small microphone, sometimes disguised under the wig or hidden at the hairline. A mic check for this microphone should take place before you have an actor put on a wig. Otherwise, you might mess up your work by

Wig caps help keep a wig clean and in place.

removing and replacing it. Coordinate this with the sound/tech department.)

Makeup usually needs to be applied before a wig goes on. (Otherwise you won't get a clean application of makeup.) You'll need to coordinate with the makeup department to give everyone time to do his or her job. The same applies to a costume that needs to go on over the head. The wig should be the costume's final touch, just to keep your hard work from getting messed up. Before the curtain goes up, double-check your **emergency kit** to make sure you have all of the necessary combs, pins, and extra wig caps. That kit will be your best friend and should never leave your side.

Remember that teamwork is doubly important on opening night. Everyone is going to be stressed, and it's important to keep a cool head. If someone seems impatient, it's probably not personal. That's just opening night stress!

Opening Night Makeup Prep

Makeup artists work alongside and coordinate with every crewmember involved in costumes and hair. Make sure that you arrive early enough to the theater to give yourself plenty of time to prepare your workspace. Once actors start to arrive, the clock will be ticking until the curtain goes up. It's important to stay on task, and the best way to do that is to be extremely organized and communicate with the other members of the crew.

When it comes to makeup, it's important to start with the most complicated, elaborate work first. Any special effects makeup that requires a lot of time to apply should be your top priority. This includes application of any prostheses or aging makeup. Time must be set aside if an actor also needs facial hair. Follow these with simpler and less time-consuming work. Experienced cast members might even apply makeup themselves. Just be sure to check in before show time for any final touch-ups.

During the Performance

Once the audience starts to arrive, someone (usually the stage manager) will alert everyone backstage that conversation will need to be kept at a lower volume. Sound carries differently in every theater. You never know what an audience member might hear. A big part of theater is creating an illusion for the audience. Overhearing conversation coming from backstage takes audience members out of a performance. During this time, actors will also want to stay backstage. The costumes, hair, and makeup in a theater production are meant to be part of the "reveal" the first time a character takes the stage.

Once the performance begins, it's up to you to keep track of your cues. You'll also want to keep an eye out for any hair and makeup issues and be ready to jump in and make a quick fix. Remember to keep your emergency kit on you at all times. However, do take time to step back and enjoy seeing your work onstage.

A Show's Run

Theater productions can run for just a few performances. Some, like highly successful and profitable Broadway productions, might run for more than a decade. As of the summer of 2017, *The Phantom of the Opera* was the longest (continuously) running production in Broadway history. (*Moose Murders*, a widely panned comedy from 1983, is among the shows that opened and closed on the same night. However, some shows have closed during preview performances, including *Breakfast at Tiffany's*

The Phantom of the Opera is the longest-running Broadway production ever.

with Richard Chamberlain and Mary Tyler Moore.) *Phantom* opened on January 26, 1988, and was still running nearly thirty years later at the Majestic Theatre in New York. During runs of that length, however, crewmembers and cast will move on. These people will be replaced as the production continues.

Runs that last a few weeks, which is typical for school and community theaters, usually retain all crewmembers for the entire run. And as time goes on, everything will start to feel instinctive. You might even start to feel relaxed before each show, knowing that you already have everything in hand. Just remember to keep on your toes. Anything can happen! This is theater, after all.

The Final Curtain

After the cast members have taken their final bows and the curtain falls on the last performance, the job isn't quite over for the crew. However, on the night of the final performance, there will likely be a party for cast and crew. This is your time to celebrate a great run, give hugs, and eat pizza! You did a terrific job.

Over the next week, you and other members of the crew will begin to clean up and put everything away. The costume shop manager will likely be in charge of coordinating cleanup in the costume shop. Any wigs that you used will need to be cleaned and stored in a place where they can be found easily for future productions. (There is usually a wig room or section in the costume shop, and by the time a show closes, you should be familiar with how it is organized.) You will also likely need to do a wig room inventory. How many wig caps are still usable? Do more need to be ordered for the future? Anything that belongs to the theater should be stored in its proper place. If you brought any supplies from home, like a curling iron or blow dryer, be sure to take them home with you. (Otherwise they might get adopted by the theater.)

If you're a freelance makeup artist who was brought in for one production, check your kit and make sure you didn't leave anything behind. Clean up your workspace and any equipment or supplies owned by the theater, and put them back where they belong.

When a production closes, crewmembers are responsible for tidying up the costume shop and putting wigs away in preparation for the next production.

Once the production has closed and your part in it is done, take some time to update your résumé to reflect your hard work. Especially if you work as a **freelancer**, keeping your résumé up to date and ready to send out for your next job is important. Also take a break and spend time with friends and family. Working in the theater can be consuming, so it's important to find time to reconnect with others. Downtime is key to getting ready to go back to work.

CHAPTER FOUR

When Things Go Wrong

Every production of every play in the history of time has faced some kind of **mishap**. If you were a part of the audience, it's possible you didn't notice at all. Perhaps a fast-thinking crewmember fixed the issue right away. Maybe you simply thought it was part of the show. Mishaps are simply a part of the theater experience, dating back to the time of Euripides. Issues can happen whether a theater company is a professional one or an amateur one. The most experienced member of a crew can make a mistake, just like anyone younger or less experienced can. Sometimes mistakes happen no matter how much time and preparation have gone into planning a show. That's theater! What you can do, as a hardworking member of the crew, is to help prevent mishaps from happening and acquire the tools to know what to do when something goes wrong.

Preparing for Anything

The most important thing you can do, no matter your role in a production, is to plan for anything and everything that can happen. How can you possibly

A makeup artist may need to give an actor a touch-up in the middle of a performance.

plan for everything? You can't. But there are things you can do to help create a safeguard against anything that can go wrong.

Have an Emergency Kit: First, always have your emergency kit at the ready. A good hair and/or wig stylist will have a pocket full of high-quality bobby pins (of various sizes and for all types and shades of hair) ready to go just in case a curl falls out of place or a wig starts to shift. A quick spritz of hairspray just might save the day. A hair stylist or makeup artist might consider investing in an apron with a large pocket or pockets to hold any number of emergency items, just in case. That way, if an actor loses a contact lens or a false eyelash, you'll be ready to help fix the problem before the next cue. A good emergency kit for a hair or wig stylist will include hairspray, bobby pins, a good wig adhesive, extra hair elastics, and a comb. Makeup artists might keep makeup removal wipes, mascara, eyeliner, powder puffs, and setting spray on hand in their emergency kits. What you add to your kit is up to you. After a little experience in the theater, you'll know exactly what you need to reach for in an emergency.

Communicate: One of the most important things you can do to keep mishaps from occurring is to make sure you're communicating with everyone. If you notice that part of a costume is missing or damaged, share that information with the members of your team and work to solve the problem. And don't limit yourself to issues that only pertain to your department. If you see an issue with a set piece, prop, or stage light, make sure you're passing that information along. Also, make yourself easy to communicate *with.* Make sure you pass your cell phone number along to those you work with most in the costumes, hair, and makeup departments, as well as to any actors you work with closely and the stage manager. Check your phone often to make sure you haven't received any emergency texts or calls. Also make sure that everyone knows who to contact if you are off site.

Stay Focused: If you're attending a rehearsal, pay attention. If you're backstage during a performance, prepping for a costume or wig change, keep an ear open for your cues, or you might miss them. It's easy to get distracted by the magic of theater and get lost in the performance, find yourself caught up in backstage drama, or get tied up in a chat with friends and cohorts. If you struggle with getting distracted easily, you might want to set reminders on your phone—just be sure to keep the phone on vibrate, especially during a performance.

Attend Meetings and Rehearsals: It's very important to stay abreast of the latest production news, so make sure you're getting to every meeting and staying to the end, even taking notes, if possible. A lot of important information gets passed along during meetings, and you don't want to miss it. If you absolutely cannot attend, make sure you talk to someone from your department who can give you the scoop afterward.

Arrive Early and Stay Late: Sometimes going the extra mile is the key to avoiding any kind of mishap, and that might mean setting aside some extra time to complete a task. Arriving twenty minutes early or staying a couple of minutes late makes you look good to anyone you work with, but it also gives you more time to complete a task. If you're feeling rushed, you are more likely to leave a task undone. Also, if you have a few moments to yourself, it's easier to organize your thoughts. When your thoughts are organized, you're not as likely to make a mistake or forget something important.

Keep a Running List of Notes: Notes are not just for meetings. Keep a production notebook and update

A LEGALLY BLONDE MISHAP

When things go wrong onstage, who is responsible for getting things back on track? Well, the answer is … anyone and everyone. According to an audience member's post on Broadway World, in a 2007 production of *Legally Blonde*, leading actress Laura Bell Bundy was performing a perfect demonstration of her character's signature "bend and snap" when her wig came off. Most wigs are pinned on carefully so that this type of thing doesn't happen, but they

Legally Blonde actress Laura Bell Bundy is no stranger to mishaps.

can become dislodged no matter how meticulous a crewmember was with the pins. An actor who is dancing or otherwise very active onstage is prone to this happening.

Actors know that a show must go on, no matter what happens. When her wig came off, the actress simply put the wig back on and continued performing while holding the wig in place. Once she was safely backstage, a member of the crew helped her to refasten the wig in place and then took precautions so that it wouldn't come loose again.

Laura Bell Bundy was no stranger to costume mishaps at the time, though. During a previous performance of *Legally Blonde*, she accidentally kicked her shoe off into the audience while dancing. Without a moment's hesitation, she simply threw off the other shoe and kept performing. An actor's ability to save face onstage is paramount to allowing the show to continue. A good-natured audience will simply play along. Meanwhile, the crew is scrambling backstage to take care of fixing the issue.

it as often as you need to. This is a good place for your meeting notes, to-do lists, ideas, or quick sketches. Staying organized is the key to avoiding mishaps, and the best way to stay organized is to keep notes on anything and everything. Date all of your notes so that if you receive a specific instruction, you can go back and see when it was delivered, if necessary.

Hair Mishaps

"You just put a bunch of pins in there and hope for the best," Stephanie Barnes said in a 2007 interview with *Playbill.* Barnes was the assistant hair and makeup supervisor for the Broadway production of *Hairspray.* The show utilized around 150 wigs, as many of the characters required more than one, and there were extras in case an **understudy** needed to go on. Five members of staff worked full-time to maintain and style the wigs for *Hairspray*, but no amount of preparation could keep character Tracy Turnblad from losing her wig. Barnes even saw wigs fall apart midshow during her time working on *Hairspray.*

When working with an actor's real hair, no amount of hairspray is too much (not just when you're working on a show called *Hairspray*). It's good to have a few different types in your arsenal: a strong-hold spray when you absolutely don't want hair to budge, and a flexible-hold spray for curls or any hairstyle that you want to be able to move naturally but still maintain its shape throughout a performance. You'll also want to make sure to keep a variety of spray around for styling wigs. There are finishing sprays that are basically hairspray for synthetic wigs.

You can use regular hairspray on wigs made from natural hair, but be sure to clean them frequently to remove any hairspray buildup. Having the right products will help you to make any necessary fix in case of a hair-mergency.

Makeup Mishaps

As a makeup artist for the theater, you'll have a kit filled with tools that will help keep makeup in place and look great throughout a performance. According

Hairspray is not only the name of a musical. It's also an important tool in any hair stylist's kit.

to an article on ThoughtCo, you can avoid any makeup issues by following a few simple rules.

1. Always use foundation, and make sure it's the right foundation. Foundation turns an actor's face into a "blank canvas," ready for makeup. Foundation evens skin tone and sets the base for powder, to prevent shine. Before applying foundation, you might want to start with a layer of barrier spray in order to protect the actor's skin.

2. Keep those hot stage lights in mind. It can be pretty easy to forget how hot it gets onstage, so be prepared with waterproof makeup, fixing spray, and a dusting of powder for a matte finish. And be ready for touch-ups with blotting papers and a powder puff! Waterproof makeup is your friend. Sweat, tears, a drink thrown in a face during a fight scene—any number of these things can lead to runny makeup.

3. Don't go light on makeup. Remember that you need actors to look good from afar, so you want to accentuate their features. If you're unsure of how much makeup to use or whether or not the finished product looks good, back up several paces and take a look. Or consult another makeup artist or member of the crew for a second opinion.

4. Keep bright colors in check and avoid heavy contrast, otherwise an actor may end up looking clown-like. Foundation with a slightly

Powdering the skin before applying eye makeup will help keep the makeup from running.

yellow tinge looks more natural from the audience, while pink can make an actor's face look too red. Again, if you aren't sure if a look is working, back up and take a look from a distance.

5. Don't skip any important steps. There is a lot of expression contained in the eyebrows, so don't forget to line them with a dark color. And don't skip the eyeliner and mascara.

Makeup is not a foolproof art. No amount of setting spray is always going to hold makeup in place under hot theater lights. An actor is going to lose a false eyelash during a dance number. An actor is going to get stinging eyeliner in his or her eyes and begin to tear up. As a makeup artist, you'll instantly know what to do to fix the problem. The trick in the theater is finding the right moment to make the fix. By the time the first performance begins, you should be familiar with all the cues and have them written out in your copy of the script. That way you'll know which actors will be backstage for a few moments, and you can do a quick touch-up or come by with your blotting papers before their next cue.

Unforeseen Circumstances

Sometimes all of the preparation in the world isn't enough to prevent a problem from occurring. And that's OK. Mistakes happen. What you do next is what's really important.

1. Let someone know.
2. Formulate a plan.
3. Make the fix.

One of the most important people involved in a stage production is the stage manager, and this person is your go-to for everything involved with the show. Stage managers are the ones who schedule and run rehearsals, oversee any work done by the stage crew, call cues during a performance, and oversee the entire show every performance. If anyone needs to know about a mishap that is occurring, it's the stage manager. (Often the stage manager will have an assistant. If you can't speak to the stage manager personally, this person is your next-best bet.) A stage manager knows all of the cues and will know the best moment for you to fix a wig or replace a missing set of eyelashes. Any fixes should take place backstage, out of the audience's view, unless there is no other way to get the job done. Work quickly and efficiently, causing the least amount of distraction as possible. Many crewmembers wear black or another dark color to avoid being seen by the audience.

Showstopper

On a very rare occasion, the show will run into an issue that prevents the performance from continuing. An actor might get injured. The electricity might go out. A member of the audience might become disruptive or run onstage. Any number of things might bring a performance to a grinding halt. If this happens, it is important to stay in communication with everyone around you. Most theaters will have the stage manager make an official announcement to the audience. Some mishaps might require a few minutes of break. Some might end the show completely. If the show is set to continue, you have to be at the ready to get right back to your cues and to help the actors get back to theirs.

If someone is dangerously injured and you are the first person on the scene, call 911 immediately, and send someone nearby to tell the stage manager what's happening. Stay with the injured person until help arrives, and follow any instructions that the stage manager gives you. You might want to familiarize

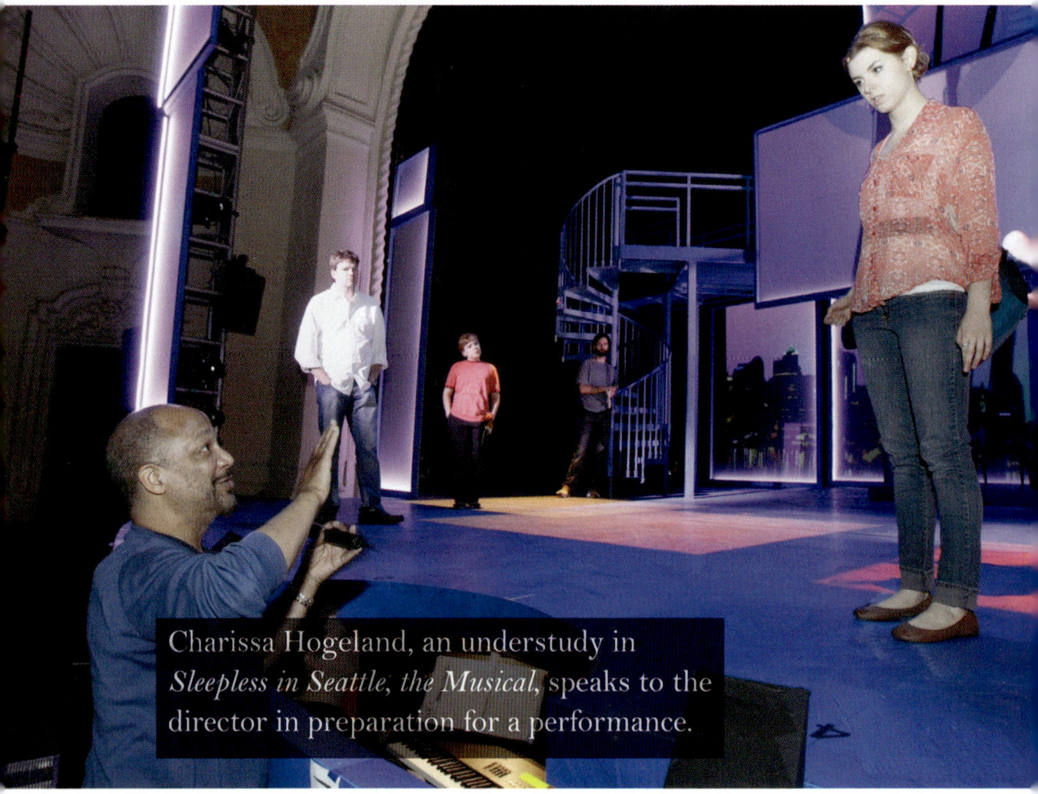

Charissa Hogeland, an understudy in *Sleepless in Seattle, the Musical,* speaks to the director in preparation for a performance.

yourself with the locations of first aid kits so that you can be prepared in case of an emergency.

If a minor injury results in an actor having to leave the show, but there is an understudy available to take his or her place, as part of the hair and makeup team you will need to be on hand in order to get the understudy ready to perform. There will almost definitely be a plan in place just in case this happens. Be ready to do your part to allow the show to continue.

If there is a fire or electrical issue, making the situation inside the theater unsafe for cast, crew, and audience members, the theater should have an evacuation plan in place. By the first night of a performance, you should be aware of all fire extinguisher locations and fire alarms. Keep a list of emergency contacts in your phone so that you won't have to search around for that emergency call sheet.

Keep Calm and Carry On

If a big mishap occurs onstage, and there is no doubt in your mind that you were the cause of it, remember that the best policy is to admit you made a mistake and move on. Mistakes, large and small, provide you with valuable experience working in the theater. The next time you are faced with a similar situation, you'll know what to do to prevent a mistake from occurring. And then, when you're interviewing for your next big theater job and the interviewer asks you how you handle a crisis, you'll have an answer at the ready.

Some hair stylists exclusively style hair in preparation for photo shoots, fashion shows, or star-studded events like awards shows.

CHAPTER FIVE

Out in the World

Before you've even finished high school, you'll start to feel that pressure of "What's next?" Soon you will be faced with a lot of big decisions about what you want to do with your future and how you can accomplish your goals. The good news is that everything you've learned working in the theater is valuable out in the real world, whether you continue on to a career in the theater or decide to try something else. Let's look at some of the career paths you might take if you love working on hair and makeup in the theater.

A Professional Hair Stylist

If you've gained some experience as a hair stylist as part of a theater production and want to continue on down that career path, you'll be pleased to know that working as a hair stylist is a versatile job in which you are often able to set your own hours, choose your own clients, and essentially be your own boss. Hair stylists can work for or own a salon; find a job in the fashion industry, styling hair for photo shoots and fashion shows; style hair for weddings or other events;

or work in the entertainment industry, styling hair for TV, movies, and theater. Some hair stylists go into style education careers, working to teach others how to style, cut, perm, and dye hair as part of the faculty of an accredited **cosmetology school**.

Many hair stylists are freelancers, meaning that they will work for a number of different clients, picking and choosing the work they would like to do as it comes. A freelance hair stylist might start the day traveling to a client's apartment for a quick cut and dye. Later that afternoon, there might be a wedding party to take care of. That night, he or she might have to style a celebrity client for an appearance at a charity gala. In short, there is no one way to be a hair stylist. Just remember that all states in the United States require you to be licensed to work as a professional hair stylist. You'll be required to take a certain number of hours of classes through an accredited cosmetology school, and then you'll have to do some hands-on training or an apprenticeship before you take the state exams. While it might seem like, "What's the big deal? It's just styling hair!" there are safety and sanitation issues that come with all branches of cosmetology that help keep you and your clients safe and free from any type of infection. You might also discover, as you begin to train for your cosmetology license, that there are a lot of things you didn't know.

Professional hair stylists must stay on top of the latest trends, but they should keep a working knowledge of hairstyles throughout history, especially if they choose a career path that takes them into the entertainment industry. Following other hair

Hair stylists who work outside of a salon can work from anywhere, even in the client's home.

stylists on social media sites like Instagram, Twitter, and Facebook will give you a great opportunity to see what everyone else in the field is doing. Creating contacts with other hair stylists will also put you one step closer to finding great gigs in the field. You might want to create your own website and social media profiles so that you can establish your brand. Websites and Instagram are great places to show off your work and generate a following.

If your passion is wigs, you don't have to work in the theater to do what you do best. Wig stylists can make and style wigs for those suffering from hair loss, including cancer patients. Wigs are also a prevalent fashion accessory for many African American women. High-quality wigs are also in demand by professional cosplayers who sometimes can't find a specific wig for a costume and might hire a professional to make one. A quality wig that looks natural, fits well, and lasts forever requires the work of a wig professional.

Hair for the Stage

It's rare for a theater to hire a full-time hair stylist, but if styling hair for the theater is what you do best, there are ways to push your career in that direction. Hair stylists who work in the entertainment industry are sometimes referred to as "entertainment hair specialists" or "theatrical hair specialists."

Many hair stylists who work in the theater are complete-package artists, trained in a variety of skills, including makeup, wigs, and special effects, as well as hair styling. There are schools that specialize in training artists specifically in styling for stage, film, and TV. As you start out, you might need to take on volunteer roles or apprentice under a more experienced stylist. Eventually, you'll be well qualified for any number of jobs in the entertainment industry. Once you've developed a good reputation and a strong client list, you can begin to choose jobs specifically in the theater, and you'll be well on your way to winning that Tony.

Professional makeup artists are often hired to do a bride's makeup for a wedding.

A Professional Makeup Artist

Many professional makeup artists are also freelancers who can choose the types of gigs they take. If your experience in the theater has put you on a path to being a professional makeup artist, you'll be able to choose your specialty and gain experience in the type of makeup art you want to do. Makeup artists might work in a salon or rent space in a few different salons, catering to a variety of clients. Some travel around, makeup kit in tow, to wherever a client is. The fashion and entertainment industries make up the largest percentage of jobs for professional makeup artists, according to Sokanu.com. Other makeup artists might style clients in preparation for a wedding or other event. It's also not uncommon for a makeup artist to do makeup part-time, while working a second job that helps pay the bills.

Full-time makeup artists might work for one specific person or company. Companies like Sephora and Ulta Beauty often hire full-time makeup artists to help sell products and give demonstrations in the store. Some of these makeup artists might represent a specific brand and give demonstrations using a particular line of products.

A very specific type of professional makeup artist works for a funeral home, preparing the deceased to be seen by friends and loved ones during their funeral. According to Chron.com, a makeup artist who works in death-care services might even make a slightly higher salary than a makeup artist who exclusively styles the living.

Says Lindsey Bacon, "I think that doing theater makeup is a great way to get a foundational understanding of makeup as a medium and a business. You get a great understanding of how lighting affects the look of makeup. You learn how to manipulate faces with shadow and highlight to create characters, age looks, and fantastical creature effects. You learn tricks to create long-lasting makeup looks that can stand up to extreme temperatures and perspiration."

Making wigs is a skill that is learned over a number of years.

MAKEUP ARTIST LINDSEY BACON

Portland-based makeup artist Lindsey Bacon started out like many professional makeup artists: with a love of theater. She says, "I got into makeup design by taking a theatrical makeup class in high school. As a child, I loved art and drawing, I performed in local and school theater, and was a total nerd for special effects from movies. But it wasn't until taking a makeup class that I realized I could put together all of the things I loved into one job."

Bacon went on to work as a freelance makeup artist for theater and film, while working a full-time job outside of makeup design. After a few years, she decided to pursue working as a makeup artist full-time. She left her full-time job to take a position at Sephora, the national makeup retail chain. Now working as a freelance makeup artist and blogger,

Makeup in the Theater

If you've been bitten by the theater bug, and you know that designing and applying makeup for the theater is your career of choice, then the good news is that you already have experience that will put you on the path toward your goals.

Many professional makeup artists who work in the theater are trained across a variety of arts. This is a great thing because a stylist with a variety of

Bacon frequently showcases her work on Tumblr, Twitter, and Instagram. She loves the business side of the business.

"As a makeup artist, you're often your own boss, so being in control of the budget and/or subject to the constraints of the budget of your theater department is helpful for learning the ropes of managing your own small business."

Bacon's experiences in theater taught her a lot about collaboration and creativity that she doesn't feel she would otherwise have learned. She says, "You learn how to manage time and workflow in a fast-paced environment while still having the room to be truly creative. You get plenty of time and repetition to practice and perfect your craft."

skills will be able to take on work with any type of show. Not every show is going to require someone who is *just* a makeup artist or *just* a wigmaker, but most shows will require someone who knows and can manage both, or even sew a button on a costume or style a **fascinator**. The longer you are in the business, however, and the more experience you gain, you will find yourself being able to be more selective about the jobs you take. And if makeup is your one true love and you want that to be your focus, then time and experience will very likely give you that ability.

Offstage Careers

Art and design is a widespread career path covering a variety of career options. If you have experience as a hair and makeup designer either in high school or college, that is a bonus on your résumé to help you land a job in a variety of professions.

Graphic Designer

A person with an eye for design might enjoy working as a **graphic designer**. Graphic designers create visual concepts for advertising, book publishing, magazines, and other mediums. They usually use design software on a computer, but some might work by hand. Graphic design involves choosing color palettes, fonts, and graphics in order to make something cohesive and intriguing to consumers. A very rare graphic designer might be self-taught through building up experience—perhaps gained through working in a theater. But most jobs in the field require at least a bachelor's degree in graphic design. Any kind of design work you've done is a valuable addition to your résumé.

Artist/Illustrator

A novice hair and makeup designer who really loves the art aspect of the work might look into building a career as an artist or illustrator. Art is a virtually boundless field of study. There are painters who work on canvas, or muralists who paint images on walls. There is sculpture and printmaking, calligraphy and collage. Illustrators create art for books and comic books. This type of art is used to tell or enhance a story.

Many artists are self-taught. Others go to art school to learn more about their craft. Some artists can make a living as an artist, selling paintings or sculptures. Others might work for specific companies, creating art for an ad campaign or comic book franchise. Being an artist requires a lot of talent and some know-how of the business side of creating and selling art.

Fashion Designer

Since hair and makeup is already a big part of creating costumes for a theater production, you might already have an established interest and experience in creating costumes. Fashion design is just one step beyond that. Fashion designers create clothing and/or accessories to be purchased and worn by the public. A fashion designer can be a hat designer or a jewelry designer, a shoe designer or a clothing designer. A designer who loves bright colors and flashy patterns will make that his or her signature style. A designer who adores classic looks, like vintage dresses, might find ways to update those classics. Fashion design is all about realizing your own style and then bringing it to life.

Beyond just creating designs for clothing, fashion designers must learn the business side—how to get

Fashion designers need to understand patterns.

publicity and create a personal brand. Fashion shows allow designers the chance to show off designs to magazines, celebrities, and company buyers.

Many fashion designers attend a fashion design school, but some might just use their sewing and design skills and begin making and selling clothing. Some designers might sell their work through sites like Etsy, hoping to be noticed by a large clothing brand.

Interior Designer or Decorator

Interior designers and decorators have an eye for living space design. Some theater experiences might give you the extra little push you need to pursue this type of career.

"Interior designer" and "interior decorator" might seem like interchangeable terms, but they are actually a little bit different. Interior designers work with architects, engineers, contractors, and others in order to create an aesthetically pleasing, safe, functional space within a building. This requires a degree, as some knowledge about architecture and building structure is necessary. Interior decorators choose accessories such as rugs, lamps, and furniture in order to "style" a room. This does not require a degree, just an eye for design and a head for business.

Your Life as a Hair and Makeup Designer

Maybe you've been bitten by the theater bug. You've styled your share of wigs. You've huddled backstage, monitoring an actor to make sure her eye makeup is holding up during her big onstage cry. You're ready to make the leap. You want to design hair and makeup professionally. Many designers are self-taught, while others might attend cosmetology school or art school or take classes to learn more about both. A hair and makeup designer might start out as a hair stylist or makeup artist, sometimes gaining valuable experience as a volunteer or in an unpaid position. One of the most important things a hair and makeup designer needs is a portfolio of past work, so be sure to photograph all of your work. Many hair and makeup designers use online portfolios for easy sharing, so technology training would not go amiss.

Your Theater Legacy

Whether your life takes you back to the theater or onto a completely different career path, the experience of working in theater is one that you will carry with you for life. It will be worth the effort, even if it just raises your makeup game or teaches you how to style the wig for your Sailor Moon costume. Or it gives you a better understanding of art, life, and how great it feels to reflect back on a job well done.

GLOSSARY

budget meeting A theater meeting that is limited to a discussion of the allocation of money in order to fund a production.

chorus A group of background performers in a musical production.

cosmetology school Also known as "beauty school," this learning institution provides classes on hair styling, skin care, cosmetics, nail care, and hair removal. A certificate from this type of school is required to become a licensed cosmetologist.

costume designer A designer who creates costume plans for a theater, movie, or television production.

costume shop A section of the theater where all of the costumes and accessories are kept, as well as any costume-making materials such as fabrics, buttons, and sewing machines.

director An individual who oversees every aspect of a theater production.

drama club A high school club in which members have a shared enjoyment of theater and often stage productions.

dress parade A rehearsal in which all characters put on their complete costumes so that the director can see all of them as a cohesive unit.

dress rehearsal A complete run-through of a theater performance, without stopping, with all actors in costume and makeup.

emergency kit A collection of items that can be easily accessed in case of a hair or makeup emergency during a performance.

fascinator A light, decorative headpiece made of beads, feathers, flowers, and other materials that is attached to a comb or hairclip.

foundation Liquid makeup that matches skin tone and provides a base coat for application of other makeup.

freelancer A person who works for several different companies, taking on individual projects, rather than working full-time for one company.

graphic designer An artist who takes colors, fonts, themes, and ideas and creates visually appealing designs in print or online for consumers.

makeup kit A collection of makeup products chosen, purchased, and used by a makeup artist.

mishap A mistake that usually becomes apparent during a performance or other activity.

playbill A program created for a theater production.

portfolio A collection of past work, used to find future work.

prostheses Scars, noses, and other features, usually made from latex, and used to create special effects for the stage.

rosacea A persistent natural redness of the facial skin.

social media Online or app-based social platforms that allow interaction, discussion, or sharing of online content.

spirit gum An adhesive specifically used to attach fake hair to faces.

technical rehearsal The run-through of a theater performance geared toward technical departments, such as lighting and sound.

touch-ups A quick repair to makeup or a hairstyle.

understudy A person who learns the role of a regular actor in a production so that he or she can take over if the actor cannot take the stage.

wig cap A nylon fabric cap that fits over the head under a wig.

FOR MORE INFORMATION

Books

Bjorklund, Ruth. *Costume Design in Theater.* Exploring Theater. New York: Cavendish Square Publishing, 2017.

Braisdell, Beverley, and Jennifer Lenard. *The Hair and Make-Up Artist's Handbook: A Complete Guide for Professional Qualifications.* London, UK: Hoddel Education, 2011.

Campbell, Drew. *Technical Theater for Nontechnical People.* New York: Allworth Press, 2016.

Davis, Gretchen, and Mindy Hall. *The Makeup Artist Handbook: Techniques for Film, Television, Photography, and Theatre.* Burlington, MA: Focal Press, 2012.

Debreceni, Todd. *Special Makeup Effects for Stage and Screen: Making and Applying Prosthetics.* 2nd ed. Burlington, MA: Focal Press, 2013.

Swinfield, Rosemarie. *Period Make-Up for the Stage: Step-by-Step.* Cincinnati, OH: Betterway Books, 1997.

Websites

DIY Finger Wave and Pin-Curl Set for Beginners
http://www.howtohairgirl.com/2012/11/diy-finger-wave-and-pin-curl-set-for-beginners
This guide for beginners provides the basics on simple curls for the stage.

How to Apply Stage Makeup
http://www.instructables.com/id/How-to-Apply-Stage-Makeup
This tutorial breaks down the basic application of stage makeup into six simple steps.

Performing Arts Supply Company
https://www.performingartssupply.com
This company stocks a variety of costume supplies for theater productions—available for sale or rent.

Stage Makeup Online
https://www.stagemakeuponline.com
This online store specializes in stage makeup and supplies.

Videos

Basic Stage Makeup Tutorial
https://www.youtube.com/watch?v=HD7t8Kivbq8
This video, from makeup artist Quirkee Q, provides a basic tutorial on applying stage makeup.

How to Do an Old Age Makeup
https://www.youtube.com/watch?v=Wq9UdaR5Cic
This quick guide shows makeup shading techniques and how they can be used to create the illusion of age.

Tutorial—Wig Roller Setting for Drag, Theater, Opera and Cosplay
https://www.youtube.com/watch?v=zg1jyYVaspE
This video tutorial provides valuable tips on styling wigs for the theater.

INDEX

Page numbers in **boldface** are illustrations. Entries in **boldface** are glossary terms.

adhesives, 37, 41, 46–48, 60
auditions, 28, 32
Avallone, Angelina, 34–35, **34**

Bacon, Lindsey, 43, 78, 80–81
Barnes, Stephanie, 64
blow dryer, 39–40, 56, **72**
Bowie, David, 10
Brand, Russell, 10
budget, 10, 13, 28–33, 36–37, 81
budget meeting, 31–32
Bundy, Laura Bell, 62–63, **62**

Cabaret, 35
chorus, 20
combs, 39, 53, 60
contouring, 44–45
cosmetology school, 74, 85
cosplay, 6, **7**, 18, 76
costume, 6, 11, 14, 16–18, 20, 24–25, 27–28, 30–36, 38–39, 42, 48–54, 56, 60, 63, 76, 81, 83, 86
costume designer, 11, 18, 20, 24, 27, 30, 32, 34–36, 48
costume shop, 32–33, 36, 56, **57**
cues, 33, 50, 54, 60–61, 68–69
curling iron, 6, 39, 56

death-care services, 78
department stores, 15, 78, 80
Depp, Johnny, 10
director, 9, 11, 18, 20, 28–29, 32, 48
drama club, 14
dress parade, 48–49
dress rehearsal, 43, 49–50

emergency kit, 53–54, 59–60
Etsy, 84
evacuation, 70–71
eyebrows, 41, 45, 67
eyeliner, 60, 67–68

facial hair, 41–42, 46, 53
fake eyelashes, 46–48, **47**, 59, 68–69
fascinator, 81
fashion design, 83–84, **84**
Fiddler on the Roof, 42

foundation, 8, 21, 45, 66–67
freelancer, 21, 56–57, 74, 77, 80

graphic designer, 82

hairspray, 59–60, 64–65
Hairspray (show), 64, **65**
hair styling
characterization and, 6, 10, 18, 20, 30, 40–41
knowledge and skills for, 12–13, 39, 74
outside of theater, 15, **72**, 73–75, **75**
preproduction and, 30–32
rehearsals and, 33, 36–41, 48–50
styling, 12, 24–25, 37–40, **40**, 51
tools for, 39–40, 42, 53, 59–60, 64
training, 15, 38–39, 85–86
troubleshooting, 59–65, 68–71
hats, 20, 32, 38, 83

Ibsen, Henrik, 24
injury, 69–70
Instagram, 75, 81
interior design, 85

Kinky Boots, **4**, 5–6

latex, 43
Legally Blonde, 62–63, **62**
Leto, Jared, 10
licensing, 21, 38, 74
lighting, 5, 16, 32–33, 43, 45, 50, 60, 66, 68, 78

makeup
applying, 11, 21–22, 44–48, **44**, **47**, 53, 66–68, **67**
characterization and, 6, 18, 20, 30, 45
history of, 8–11, 35, 46–47
knowledge and skills for, 8–12, 21, 43–44
outside theater, 15, 21, 77–78, **77**, 80–81
preproduction and, 30–32
rehearsals and, 33, 42–43, 48–50
removing, 11, 22, 46
special effects, 18, 20–21, 35, 42–43, 48, 53, 78
training, 8–11, 21, 43, 80, 86–86
troubleshooting, 59–61, 64–71
makeup kit, 21, 46, 56, 65, 78
mascara, 47, 60, 67
meetings, 18, 20, 27, 30–33, 39, 50, 61, 64
microphones, 22, 24, 51–52
mishap, 58, 60–64, 68–71
moisturizer, 11, 45–46

Peking Opera, 11
performance rights, 28
permit, 15
Phantom of the Opera, The,

20–21, 54–55, **55**
pins, 6, 22, 28–29, 39, 53, 59–60, 62–64
playbill, 14
Porter, Billy, **4**, 5–6
portfolio, 21, 41, 49, 86
powder, 45, 48, 60, 66
producer, 25, 29
prostheses, 20–21, 35, 42–43, 48, 53

research, 12, 31, 35, 39, 46–47
résumé, 57, 82
rosacea, 8

salons, 15, 73, 77
scar, 42, 48
set, 11, 14, 20, 28, 60
setting spray, 45, 48, 60, 68
skin care, 8, 21–22,
skin tone, 8, 44–45, 66
social media, 14, 75, 81
sound, 50–52
spirit gum, 41
state manager, 30, 32, 54, 60, 68–69
straightening iron, 39

technical rehearsal, 50
Thespis, 10–11
time management, 26–27
Tony Awards, 5, 76
touch-ups, 47, 53, 66, 68
Tutankhamun, King, 10

understudy, 64, 70, **70**

weddings, 21, 73–74, **77**, 78
Wicked, 16, **17**
wig cap, 22, 51, **52**, 53, 56
wigs
  fitting, 22, 36, 51–53
  maintaining, 12, 24, 64–65
  storing, 13, 56, **57**
  styling, 6, 12, 22, 36, **37**, 38, 51, **52**, 64, 76

ABOUT THE AUTHOR

Bethany Bryan is an author, hair and makeup enthusiast, and comics editor. She wrote *Set Design and Prop Making in Theater* for a previous set in this Exploring Theater series. Her love of musical theater began with *The Sound of Music* and continues today. She lives in Kansas City, Missouri.